Options Trading

Powerful Beginners Guide to Dominate Stocks

Table Of Contents

Introduction 3

Chapter 1: Options Trading Basics and Concepts 7

Chapter 2: The Advantages 22

Chapter 3: Types of Options...27

Chapter 4: Understanding Risk...34

Chapter 5: Strategies and Techniques...41

Conclusion...45

Introduction

I want to thank you and congratulate you for buying the book, "Options Trading".

Why does Options Investing Appeal to People?

Any type of investing is appealing to the average person because it hints at promises of financial freedom, the ability to do what you want when you want to (instead of being tied to a job at all hours of the day) and possibly even early retirement. However, if this were an easy thing to do, everyone would be an investor. So, what makes this subject so complicated, and what is the best way around that?

This book contains proven steps and strategies on how to understand the world of options trading. Many people are intrigued by investing, but aren't sure where to start with learning about it. In this guide, you will learn the basic concepts behind it, the terms most commonly used, and more. When you are done reading this guide, you should have an idea of whether or not options trading is right for you. You can then decide to pursue the subject with certainty.

Common Options Trading Concepts to Learn:

Reading about options trading can be intimidating and overwhelming. This is largely due to the fact that literature or articles on the subject use words that you are not familiar with. In this book, we will cover a fair amount of the common terms used in options trading, so you can feel better prepared to tackle this subject with confidence.

How Risky is it to get Involved with Trading Options?

Some people believe that options trading comes with less risk than other areas of investing, and this is true, to a certain degree. However, since each area of investment comes with its own unique set of risks, dangers, and rewards, the only way to figure out which is best for you is to become as knowledgeable as you can. This book will help you do that. After reading it, you can make a choice about which investment style will best suit your life.

Thanks again for buying this book, I hope you enjoy it!

are for clarifying purposes only and are the owned by the owners themselves, not affiliated with this document.

Chapter 1: Options Trading Basics and Concepts

In our present day, a lot of portfolios of investors include material on stocks, bonds, and mutual funds. But the different types of securities you can access are not simply limited to those items. There is another type that exists which is known as options, and this gives investors a whole new level of opportunity. Similar to what the name of this type of investing hints at, this field will give you plenty of options, instead of tying you to one line of action or thought.

One of the best things about options trading is the versatility involved. We all have busy lives or varying lifestyles, and there is no "one size fits all" method when it comes to investing. With options trading, you can enjoy this reality without stress. You can adjust and adapt the position you take in accordance with any situation that may come up. What this means is that you can do anything from protecting your positions against declines to banking on motions of the market.

Options Trading Disclaimers and Warnings:

This sounds great on the surface, and it is, but the versatility of options does come with its own unique set of costs. Options trading is a complex and, at times, risky endeavor to become involved in. That's why you will encounter disclaimers, while trading, warning about risks and mention that options are not suitable for all people. These disclaimers will also mention that options are extremely speculative and that you should only invest with money you can afford to lose.

So, no matter what anyone says to the contrary, options trading does involve plenty of risk, but this risk is magnified many times over when you aren't knowledgeable about the subject. Due to this fact, a lot of people will suggest that you should stay away from options trading altogether and forget they even exist. However, staying ignorant about any investment type puts you in a weaker position than you need to be in. It's possible that the speculative quality of this type of trading simply isn't your thing. There's no issue there, it just means that you shouldn't partake in speculating with options.

What you are Missing Out on by Staying Away from Options:

Before you jump the gun and make the decision to refrain from investing in this type of trading, you should at least have an understanding of how they work. Being unaware of the way options work is just as dangerous as diving in headfirst without enough knowledge. Not being aware of how options function means that you are not only limiting yourself from diversifying your investment experience, but you would also lose out on valuable insight into the way the largest corporations in the world function. From handing some ownership over to employees with stock options, to hedging foreign exchange risks, nearly all multi-national corporations utilize options trading in some way.

What, Exactly, are Options in Options Trading?

This chapter will get you acquainted with the fundamental basics of options trading. Remember, though, that most traders in this area of investment have a lot of experience and that expecting to become an expert right away is silly. So, what does the word "options" refer to in options trading? The option is a contract that allows a buyer to have rights to sell or buy assets at a particular price, either before a date or on a date. However, this right does not obligate them. These options, similar to bonds or stocks, are securities, and also count as contracts that have properties and terms that have been defined specifically and strictly.

If you are still confused, it may help to think of this in different terms. The concepts behind these options are there in many situations of an everyday nature. For example, say that you have found a home that you want to buy; but you aren't going to have enough money to purchase it for at least a few months from now. You may still wish to buy this home since it appears to be perfect, the home of your dreams, and everything you've been hoping and wishing for. Instead of accepting the fact that you simply don't have the capital to make this purchase, you have another option.

You have a chat with the seller and work out a deal that allows you the option to purchase the house in a few months for a specific price. The seller allows you to do this, but you have to pay a price for it. Now, think of these situations that could possibly occur.

Getting Extra Value from the Unexpected Detail:

You find out that the home is actually a famous person's birth house. This causes the value of the house to grow in a huge way. Since the seller sold that option to you already, he has to sell the home to you for the amount you agreed upon. This means that you make a huge profit from the house.

Changing your Mind about the Purchase:

Now consider this alternative theoretical scenario. While getting to know and exploring the home, you find out that there is asbestos filling the walls and that the basement is full of rats. Even though you, at first, were under the impression that you had found the perfect home, you aren't interested in it anymore and see no value in the house. The positive side of this is that you aren't obligated to finalize the sale, since you purchased the option. However, you did pay for that option and don't get that money back.

The Important Points Demonstrated Above:

These examples show two points that are highly important about options. First, when you purchase one, you earn a specific right, but aren't obligated. It's up to you to allow the date to go by, allowing the option to lose all of its value. When this occurs, you lose all of what you invested (the money you put down to have that option). Secondly, options are just contracts meant to represent underlying assets. Typically, these are indexes or stocks.

Two Options Types; Puts and Calls:

2. Calls: There are two types of options. The first is a call, which allows the holder a right to purchase assets at specific prices and in a specific time period. These are very similar to taking the long position with stocks. People who purchase calls do so in hopes that their stock will rise in value significantly before their option gets past its expiration date.

3. Puts: The second type of options is a put. This allows a holder rights to sell off assets at a specific price by a specific time period. These are similar to taking the short position in stocks. People who buy puts do so in hopes that their stock price will go down before the expiration date of their option.

Who Participates in the Market of Options?

Depending on their position, there are usually four participant types in the markets of options trading. These are either buyers or sellers of calls, and buyers or sellers of puts. The ones who purchase options are known as holders and the ones who sell them are known as writers. In addition to this, buyers are known as having what is called long positions, while the sellers are known to operate using short positions.

Buyers and Sellers; An Important Difference:

Holders (either call or put) have no obligation to sell or buy. They can exercise choice, if that is what they want to do. Sellers (either call or put), on the other hand, are under an obligation to sell or buy. What this means is that sellers may have to fulfill an agreement they made to either sell or buy. This may seem very confusing now, as it does to everyone at first. That is why we will be looking at options trading from the buyer's point of view. Taking the selling position with options is a lot more complex and possibly, in some cases, a lot riskier. Right now, it's enough to have an understanding of the fact that there exist two different sides to contracts that involve options.

Options Trading Concepts:

When you get into trading options, you have to be aware of the concepts used to describe the market and other details about it:

-Strike Price: The strike price refers to the underlying stock's price to be either bought or sold at. This value is what a stock has to either go over or under before the specific position is profitable, which needs to happen before the date of expiration.

-The Listed Option: A listed option is typically on options exchanges on a national level. They usually have a strike price that is fixed and also set dates of expiration.

- **The Premium:** This refers to the entire cost of an option, and can be determined by looking at qualities, such as the strike price, value of the stock, the time left until it expires, and how volatile it is. Considering each of these, figuring out an option's premium is complex.

A Couple of Main Reasons an Investor would Choose Options Trading:

Different styles of investing are good for different reasons, and the main reasons for choosing options can be pinned down to a couple of main categories:

- For the Reason of Speculation:

Consider speculation as a way to bet on a security's movement. One of the plus sides of options trading is not being limited to profiting just when the market is moving upward. Due to their versatility, options can let you earn profit no matter which direction the market happens to be heading.

A lot of money is made in speculation, but a lot of money is also lost here. People using options like this are one of the reasons they have such a risky reputation. That is due to the fact that when someone purchases an option, they must be right in predicting which direction that stock will head, along with how big it will get and the timeline of the entire motion. For this to work, you have to predict correctly whether stocks will head upward or downward, while also being correct about the amount of price change and the timeframe for this to occur. You also have to keep commission in mind, meaning the odds are against you even more.

Looking at all of this, you may wonder why people choose speculation for options trading. But apart from how versatile they are, leverage is also a big plus. Having many shares under just one contract means that even slight movements can earn you big money.

- The Reason of Hedging: Another function of choosing to trade options is something called hedging, which can be compared to a policy for insurance. Similar to the way you insure a car or house, options can insure investments against downward trends in the market. People who criticize this trading method claim that you should not invest if you are so uncertain of the stock you chose that you require hedging.

However, there's a lot of doubt about strategies for hedging being useful, particularly when it comes to bigger institutions. Investors on an individual level can profit as well. Say you are interested in taking advantage of the stocks in technology and their upward motions, but are looking to limit your losses. Using options is a good way to lessen the risks of downward trends, while still gaining benefits from the upsides in a way that is quite cost effective.

Stock options for employees are not available to all of us, but this particular class of option would be considered another good reason to use options. A lot of companies utilize options as a method for attracting and keeping employees who are talented, particularly in regards to management. These are similar to typical stock options since they give holders a right to purchase stock in a company, but it does not obligate them. However, the contract exists between the company and the older, in contrast to normal options that exist as contracts between two entities that have nothing to do with the business.

Trading Out versus Exercising:

We have briefly covered options as the choice to either sell or buy (also known as exercise). Although this does apply, most options are not utilized in this way. In other words, most of the options are not exercised. You could either make a profit by exercising at a certain amount and then selling stock off at a higher amount to earn that way. Or, you could hold onto the stock with the awareness that you bought it at a discounted price.

Typically, holders select the option of taking their profit by using a method of trading (or closing) out. What this means is that they sell off their options to other people on the market, then writers purchase them to close. Statistics say that about 10 percent of options are actually exercised, with 60 percent being traded, and 30 percent expiring with their value lost.

Time Value and Intrinsic Value:

Right now, more details about how options are priced should be explained. At times, options fluctuate in price, which is the result of time value along with intrinsic value. In essence, the premium of an option equals its time value plus its intrinsic value. Keep in mind that what intrinsic value means is the "in the money" amount, meaning the stock's price is equal to the strike price. What time value means is the chance that the option may go up in value. How this ends up working out is that options typically end up trading above their intrinsic value amount.

Some Information about Adjustments in Options Trading:

Adjustments refer to change in the terms of a contract because of corporate actions (like a stock split or a merger). Dependent on what corporate action is chosen, differing terms for the contract (like the date of expiration, strike price, multiplier, and more) might get adjusted accordingly. An option that has been adjusted might cover either less or more of its usual amount of 100 shares.

Now that we have gone over some options trading basics, you might find it helpful to learn about some terms that you will hear over and over again when researching or, in any way, dealing with options trading.

Options Trading Concepts to Learn and Commit to Memory:

-American Style Option: This refers to an option that is able to be exercised whenever the investor wishes, as long as it is before the option's date of expiration. We will talk more about this later on in the book, as well as the difference between an American style option and a European style option.

-The Competing or Market Maker System: This is a technique for offering liquidity in the market for options trading, by keeping the market makers in a state of competition with each other. This is a possible alternative choice for specialist systems that also has the responsibility of conducting orderly and fair markets within a specific options class.

-Open Interest: This refers to the complete amount of option contracts that are outstanding for a certain stock that is underlying or in a specific series.

-Market Quote: Refers to the quotations of current ask prices or bid prices for particular stocks or options on the trading floor of an exchange, or in the market. The investor will then typically get their information from a firm that uses brokerage. But these quotes are highly disseminated, for stocks or options that are listed, and can be accessed with different quotation services that work with commercial material.

-Open Outcry: A method for trading that involves market makers competing and brokers on the floor standing for orders that are public. The two groups will make offers and bids right on the floor of trading.

- **Arbitrage in Trading**: This is a method technique for trading that has to do with purchasing and selling, at the same time, equivalent or identical assets. This is done in a couple of different markets, and done with an intention of earning profit due to the discrepancy in price.

- **The Point of Breaking Even (or Break Even point):**

This refers to the price of a stock, at the point that it doesn't result in a loss, but also doesn't result in a profit. The point of break even in a strategy is usually given along with the date of expiration, but the break-even point can also be determined, for dates outside of this, by an option model for pricing that is more theoretical.

-**Broker:** This refers to an individual who works as the agent of conducting securities exchanges or transactions; the broker or account executive who handles communicating with customers directly at the brokerage firm. It is someone who works on trading floors as a floor broker, works in an exchange and is the one executing other people's orders for trading.

-**Discount:** This word, in options trading, is basically the same as its definition in other areas. A discount refers to options that are trading below their intrinsic value price. In other words, they trade below their parity.

-**Exercise Amount for Settlement:** This term refers to the difference in the index's exercise value for settlement and the option's exercise price that is being exercised on the same day the index option is being exercised.

- **Intrinsic Value:** A portion, known as "in the money", of the premium of an option.

- Expiration Cycle: This refers to the dates of expiration that can apply to differing options series. Usually, there are three different types.

- Listed Option: This is a call or a put that is traded using an options exchange that is national. As opposed to this, options that are "over the counter" typically have terms that are not standard or have been negotiated.

- Long Option Position: This refers to the position an owner or purchaser of options has that stands for a right to either sell off stock (when a put happens), or purchase stock (when a call happens) at a specific price (known as a strike price), either on a specific date or before that date (date of expiration). This position will occur when an opening purchase exchange (long put or long call) happens.

-Long Stock Position: A long stock position refers to the position of an investor having bought and owning stock.

-Margin Requirement or Margin: This is the lowest amount of equity needed to support a position for investment. If you are buying on margin, you are borrowing from a brokerage firm a portion of the price of purchase, of a security.

- Market to Market: Market to market refers to the process for accounting when the price of securities being held in a particular account are priced every day in order to reflect quotes from the closing market or the closing prices. This can result in the equity being updated very often, in an account, in order to properly reflect the security prices at that current time.

- Opening Transaction: This is something that gets added to or created as a position for trading. Purchasing transactions, at their opening, add a lot of long options to the main total position of any investor. A transaction that occurs at the opening of the sale will include options that are short. A transaction that occurs at the opening of an option will add to the open interest of the option.

- Market Order: A market order is an order for trading that is placed using a broker to sell or purchase an option or stock at the most quality price possible or available.

- Physical Delivery: This type of option is an option that has a commodity or physical good as the underlying asset or entity. This can mean either a foreign currency or a common stock choice. When the owner of this option fulfills or exercises it, a delivery of the commodity or good takes place, being transferred from one account for trading or brokerage, to another account.

- Stop Order: Refers to a type of order of contingency, which some refer to mistakenly as a stop-loss, put in with a hired broker. This will turn into a market order once a trade for the stock takes place, when it's offered or bid, at certain, agreed on prices.

- Market Maker: A market maker is a member of the exchange that works on a trading floor and sells or purchases options on their own behalf, for their personal account. This means that they have a responsibility to make offers and bids to maintain an orderly and fair market. This is related, as well, to a specialist or specialist group.

- Discretion: This refers to the freedom given to an account executive, by the investor, to use their own judgment when it comes to fulfilling or executing orders. This is usually limited, such as the example of limit orders that allow the broker on the floor to enjoy a flexible state beyond the limit price that has been stated to use their own judgment with fulfilling that order. However, discretion can be unlimited as well, such as the example of an order that is "market not held".

- Early Exercise: This is a quality of American style trading that lets an owner use (or exercise) their option. This applies no matter when they wish to do so, as long as it is before the date of its expiration.

- **European Style Options:** These are options that are able to be fulfilled (or exercised), before their date of expiration, but only when it's a certain period of time.

- **Technical Analysis:** Future stock prices and their motions can be predicted using this method of analysis, which has to do with studying data from markets in a historical way. This includes actual prices, the volume of trading, interest, the volume of short selling, and the relation of decline in issues to the advancement.

- **Averaging Down:** This refers to the act of purchasing more of an option or stock at a price that is lower than the original amount, in hopes of lowering the overall average of the options or stocks.

- **Bear Spread in Options:** This refers to one of a varying group of strategies used that involve at least two options (or more). This can also mean options that have been mixed in with positions dealing with the underlying stock, which may profit from a lowering of the underlying stock's falling price.

-**Exercise Price:** This refers to the price an option's owner can either sell (put) or buy (call) a stock that is underlying. This can be used in place of strike price or strike, since they mean essentially the same thing.

-**Option Period:** This refers to the time starting from when a writer or buyer of the option makes up a contract for that option, to the date that it expires. This can also be called, accurately, the lifetime of an option.

-**Over the Counter:** This is an association of a decentralized participant in the market, similar to an exchange with many of its qualities, allowing trades to happen over electronic exchanges rather than a physical location or trading floor.

-Ask Price or Ask: This definition simply refers to a price set for a stock or an option, by the seller.

-Bid Price or Bid: This refers to the amount that a buyer will purchase a stock or option.

-Parity: A word that means the contract of an option's complete premium, as long as that premium is worth as much as the intrinsic value of it. For an example, options can be known as worth parity when they are being traded only for their value intrinsically. You can measure parity against the last bid, offer, of sale of a stock.

- Payoff Diagram: This refers to a chart of losses and profits of a specific strategy for options which is created ahead of time, before a strategy gets executed. It's a plot of the profits that are expected to occur or the losses that may happen against an underlying security's value and price.

-Market or Stock Volatility: This is a measure of the fluctuation of stock prices. Volatility is mathematically the standard deviation, in an annualized way, of the changes of a stock price on a daily level.

- Bearish: This is a word used in investments to describe an option of a stock going down in price. This could also refer, in general, to the market and is typically thought of as a pessimistic or negative attitude to have.

- Overwrite: An overwrite is a strategy for an option that has to do with writing (either partially or wholly) call options up against long positions of stock that already exist. This is not the same as a buy-write type of method that has to do with purchasing stock and writing calls at the same time.

- Beta: This refers to the measurement of the way individual stock movements stay with the overall movements of the stock market.

- Writer or Write: This refers to selling options that are not owned, using a method of a transaction that is opening sale. As the just described position stays open, a writer can fulfill the contract's option obligations (whether it be selling off the stock if call happens, or purchasing the stock if a put happens), if the option itself gets assigned. Investors who end up selling off options are known as writers, whether an option is uncovered or covered.

Chapter 2: The Advantages

Options that operated on exchanging trading began back in the 1970s. However, this type of investment has grown in popularity a lot more in our modern times. Data gathered by the Board of Options Exchange in Chicago revealed that the amount of contracts traded in options, in America, was a little over 500 million in 1999. Just seven years later, it grew to over two billion. What contributed to this surge in popularity for options trading? You will find out in this chapter.

It's true that they have come to be known as dangerous and risky investments, only understood by the most expert of traders, but options are also, in certain circumstances, useful to the average everyday investor. In this chapter, we will review the unique advantages offered in options trading and the benefits they can give to your investment journey and portfolio.

Options Trading Advantages:

Options have been around for over three decades, but are only now beginning to receive the attention they have always deserved. A lot of different investors have stayed away from options trading, thinking that they are too sophisticated, complex, and difficult to follow for the average person. Others have experienced negative results because they either had brokers who didn't understand what they were doing, or did not have enough knowledge themselves to be involved in the field quite yet. Using options improperly, similar to any other powerful resource is a recipe for disaster. Having a bad first experience is enough to scare people into swearing off of something, even if that thing has great potential when used widely.

In addition, descriptions like "dangerous" or "risky" have been unfairly applied to options trading by people involved in the market or financial media outlets. Every investor who invests on an individual level should make sure that they are getting all sides to each story before they make a judgment about an investment type. The major advantages given to investors by deciding on options trading are of the following: improved cost efficiency, numerous alternatives structured in a strategic fashion, and the potential to give larger returns to investors. There is less risk involved, at times, than equities.

Looking at this considerable list of advantages to options, you can understand why people would desire to use this avenue and might have trouble coming up with a reason as to why they haven't been very popular in older times. Let's review these options benefits:

- Better Cost Efficiency with Options:

There is a lot of amazing leveraging power present in options. Investors can get positions that copy positions in stock very similarly, but in a much more cost efficient way.

- They are not as Risky:

This, of course, depends entirely on the way you decide to use options. In some scenarios, opting for options is more dangerous than deciding to own equities. However, there will also be scenarios when options are useful for reducing risk. This all depends entirely on the way you use options. They can be less dangerous for individuals who invest, due to the fact that they don't need as much commitment financially as equities. They can be less dangerous, because of their safety (relatively speaking) against potential negative or devastating results of gap openings.

Options trading is the most dependable way to use hedge methods, which means that they are also safer than most stock options out there. Whenever someone buys stock, there are frequently stop loss orders attached with the purpose of protecting their position. This is meant to stop losses under a decided upon price decided by the person doing the investing.

The issue here is within the very nature of these orders. Stop orders are applied when stocks trade either below or at the limit decided within the order ahead of time.

If you had gone the route of buying the put option ahead of time to protect yourself, you wouldn't have suffered a devastating loss. Options, unlike orders of the stop loss variety, don't close down when the market does. Instead, they allow you to have insurance all hours of the day and night, every day of the week; another feature that stop orders cannot compete with. For this reason, options are, according to many, considered dependable as a hedging form.

In addition, instead of buying the stock, it's possible to have employed a method that involves buying calls that are "in the money", rather than buying the stock on its own. Options exist out there that will copy over 80 percent of the performance of a stock, but will charge a price that is equal to one fourth of the stock price. If it turns out that you had bought a strike call rather than buying a stock, the losses you suffer would only be what you had spent on your option. How effective stop orders are is nothing compared to full time, natural stops that options offer investors.

-Better Return Potentials:

A calculator is not necessary to discover that if you don't spend as much capital and earn the same amount of money, you will have higher returns in money. When these end up paying off, this is what is offered to investors by options.

-A Better Variety of Alternatives:

Another huge advantage to options trading is the fact that they give you a lot more alternatives for investing, due to being so flexible. This means that there are lots of ways you can utilize options to create alternative, similar positions. These positions are referred to as synthetics.

These synthetic types of positions give people who invest many different methods for attaining similar goals for investment, which turns out to be highly useful to them. Although these positions are usually considered quite advanced when it comes to options, there are a lot of strategic alternative options. Also, this is a subject you can get to know as you become well-versed in the world of options trading.

An example of good alternatives in regards to this is that investors can utilize brokers who charge margins when other investors try shorting their stocks. The margin requirements here, and their cost, can be very limiting. Some investors, on the other hand, utilize brokers who do not make room for the possible shorting of certain stocks. Not being able to handle or deal with the downsides of stocks when they are necessary, in essence, holds investors back and makes them stay in a world that is limited by black and white, as the world of the market is full of colors. However, there is not a single broker out there that has principles against buying puts to take advantage of downsides, and this is yet another advantage of getting into the world of trading options.

Using options trading also lets investors trade on what is called the "third dimension" of the market, which can also be thought of as having no direction at all. Options trading will let someone who invests trade based on movements of stock, and also the amount of time that passes and volatility shifts. The majority of stocks do not move in large ways the majority of the time, or at least not on a regular basis. There are only a small number of stocks that make significant moves like this, and this only occurs once in a blue moon (very rarely). The ability you have to use this type of lack of motion could end up being what determines how good you are at this game. It could be a factor that has a lot to do with whether you reach your money goals or simply dream about them and never get the chance to see them happen. Options trading is the only type of investing that allows you to use the alternatives that are necessary in a strategic fashion, allowing you to earn profits, no matter what the market type you are dealing in is.

When you look over the main pros and benefits of trading with options, it can seem obvious why they are such a popular investment choice in circles of finance these days. Considering the fact that brokerages on the internet give people access, directly, to the markets of option trading online and with extremely low fees and costs to get involved, retail investors, on average, can utilize their ability to take advantage of great tools. These involve powerful methods for the industry of investment, similar to the way the best of the best investors do. This means you should take it upon yourself to spend a lot of time learning the ropes.

Have Respect for the Learning Process:

Take the time to learn how to use options trading methods in the right way. This will provide you with countless benefits, amazing skills, and more to add to your portfolio. This will also help you with exploring other areas of investing and trading, even if they are unrelated to options trading. This will help you be on your way to financial freedom.

Chapter 3: Types of Options

In the world of options trading, there exist two main categories of options trading types to consider. These are American options and European options. In this segment, we will cover the distinct features of each, along with their similarities.

American Style Options:

These are options that can be taken advantage of (exercised) at any given moment, as long as it is in between the purchase date and the date of expiration. The majority of options that are exchanged fit in this category.

European Style Options:

These types of options differ from the American variety since they are only allowed to be used (or exercised) when they are nearing the end. Although it sounds that way on the surface, the differences between European and American options are not related to geography. There are four main distinctions that can be made between these two types of options.

The Differences between American and European Style Options:

All stocks that come with options and ETFs (exchange traded funds) involve options that are American style. In larger indices, there are only a few indices that involve options that are American style, like the S&P 100. Larger indices have options that are actively traded using European style options, like the S&P 500.

- Index Options Trading: Options for American style trading stop when businesses close down, in the month of expiration, on the third Friday of that month. However, there are some option styles that are known as quarterlies, allowing people to trade up until the very last day, of the last quarter of the calendar, for trading. There are also weekly options which end their trading during a specific week, on the Friday of that week.

- The Price for Settlement: This refers to the closing price, officially, for a period of expiration and also determines the in the money options along with options that need to be exercised using auto-exercise methods. Options that are in the money by at least one cent by the date of expiration automatically become fulfilled (or exercised). The exception to this is the owner of the option requesting specifically that their broker does not do this.

- Exercising Rights: People who own options that are American style are allowed to exercise their option(s) at any given moment in time, as long as it is before the expiration date, but people who own options that are European style can only do this at the date of expiration. Index options for European style trading end their trading a day earlier, as a business closes, not on Friday, but the Thursday before that third Friday.

On each third Friday for that particular month, every stock receives a price that it will open with on the index. Since they have different opening times, a few of the prices for opening get decided at 9:30 in the morning (Eastern time), with others being determined a short while after. Others won't start trading for as long as a couple of hours after.

An index price, in the underlying sense, is determined just as though all of the stocks were being traded simultaneously, at the respective prices for opening that were determined for them. This price says nothing about the stock's price in a real world sense, since it's impossible to view index prices that are published and operate under the assumption that its price for settlement is a similar value to the prices that were published in the index in the early morning hours.

- More about Exercising Rights: As soon as you are the owner of a certain option, you hold a right to exercise the option. Every once in a while, it might be to your benefit to do this before the expiration date, especially if you have a dividend to collect, however, it's rarely ever that important. When you end up being short on your option that is American style (meaning that you sold it off but did not own it) and receive a notice to exercise before its expiration date, you won't be missing the option, but instead missing the stock.

- If Account Size is an Issue: This is no issue, unless you have too small of an account to carry a position that is short with the stocks. If this is the case, you should reconsider options trading until your account has grown.

- An Extra Risk for American Style Trading: There is a significantly higher risk with early assignments that happen in a cash settled fashion with American style index options trading, and this pretty much only occurs in that area. For this reason, the best way to get rid of risks that come with early exercising is staying away from American style options altogether.

When it comes to getting notices for assignments early on in the day, you have to rebuy the option at a price that is equal to the intrinsic value of the night before. This may put you in a risky situation if substantial moves occur in the market. That is because the purchase you were forced to make alters the position you hold and makes it significantly different than the one you believed you held.

- Settling Options using Cash: Everyone benefits when this is how options are settled. For American style, the price of settlement for whatever the underlying asset is (index, ETF, or stock) is the closing price in a regular sense, or the final trade as the market is closing on the Friday we mentioned earlier. Trades that happen after hours don't come under consideration when the price for settlement is being determined.

For the European style, learning what the settlement price will be is not as easy. Actually, this information won't get published for a while (sometimes a few hours) after the trading market has opened. Since the options that are settled with cash are nearly always of the European variety, and these assignments only happen when there is expiration, the cash value of an option gets decided by the price of the settlement.

- The Price for Settlement: In options that are American style, there are far less surprises to take into account. If you see the price of a stock being traded before it expires on Friday, you can safely assume that the number of puts associated with it will pass their expiration date and be worthless and that the number of calls will end up, reliably, in the money. If you have taken a position that is short and wish to not get assigned a notice for exercise, you have the option to buy the calls again.

The price for settlement may be different, and the calls might change from "in the money" to "out of the money". However, you aren't likely to see much of a value change in the closing last minutes. With options that are European style, the price for settlement is very hard to predict and often is surprising. This means that it could be advantageous to some and disastrous for others. This is due to the fact that in the morning, when the market first opens up to traders, there might be a notable price difference from the close the night before.

Not that this is very common or occurs often, but it does enough for the idea of an overnight hold on a position to suddenly seem risky and dangerous, at times. When the European style option is yours, you will see a likely scenario on the afternoon before the market closes, right before your stock expires. None of the shares will exchange or change hands. This means you don't need to be worried about starting over on your portfolio.

You will not be losing stocks if you get a notice for exercise on previously written calls, like collar strategies or call writing that is covered. The owner of the option is the one who will get the cash, and the one selling will pay the value of said option. This amount equals the intrinsic value of the option. If it turns out the option has no money, it has no value and will pass its expiration date completely worthless.

What Happens when the Option is Short?

This is a unique challenge with different considerations to take into account. If you find that your option is nearly worth nothing, holding it anyway and wishing for a big turnaround is not the worst idea possible. People who own options that are low priced, meaning that they are worth 15 cents or less, have earned up to hundreds or thousands of dollars, due to the gapping open of the market the next morning. The majority of the time, their options end up passing the expiration date and becoming completely worthless, but sometimes, a huge reward can happen.

Let's say you own an option with a decent value. This means you have an important choice that needs to be made. The price for settlement could end up making your option completely worthless, or take the opposite turn and go up in value times two. Is this a risk you are willing to take? There is no right answer here and it's a choice that all individuals who invest must make on their own.

American Style vs. European Style Options Summary:

If you do decide that index option trading is something you want to do, you must be sure that you are aware of the important distinctions between the European style and American style. Even more crucial than this, to get away from the chance of losing significantly, you need to realize how European option prices for settlement get decided and how they function. This will make a large difference in the way a position is managed by you, particularly when this position has to do with short options, as well. It's important to avoid risks that come along with settlement by utilizing the option to exit positions that don't have much more for you to benefit from. This should be done by Thursday at the latest, which will be the very last day you can trade the options.

Options for Long Term:

Thus far, we've gone over how options work in a context of the short term. It may go without saying that there are options that have a holding time of up to many years. These could be more suitable for investors who are interested in long term choices. This completely depends, of course, on individual considerations, capital, and lifestyle. These are known as LEAPS (or long term equity anticipation securities). These options give opportunity to manage and control risk, also the chance to speculate, so in this way they are the same as your typical options. However, LEAPS give chances for time periods that are a lot longer than the typical options. Even though they aren't a choice for every stock, LEAPS can be found on most popular or well- known issues.

Exotic Options Information and Considerations:

The basic puts and calls we have gone over are called vanilla options, by some. Although information about options trading can be hard to follow when you first start reading about it, the plain vanilla variety of options are as simple as it can get. Due to how versatile options are, in general, there are a wide variety of types out there. The options that are not standard are known as exotic, meaning they can be either the plan vanilla type with varied details on profiles for payout, or different material altogether with extra options-like details added on.

Chapter 4: Understanding Risk

Of course, no type of investment comes without some measure of risk or danger. Options trading is, of course, included in this generalization. When you become aware of this risk, you can be well on your way to becoming a fantastic trader who enjoys success on a regular basis. The best way to become aware of what this risk means, and get on top of it and benefit from protecting yourself against it, you should find out as much as you can about it.

What Draws People into Options Trading?

A lot of people who invest get extra excited about going into trading options because of the leverage involved in investments that are successful. It's true that some stock investors can make up to 20 percent profit (returns) on any given stock. But options traders can make, potentially, up to 1,000 percent, and this is all within the same time period. These types of profits are possible due to the fact that options trading offers a lot of leverage. Someone who is highly skilled and adept at options trading knows that they can have control over the same amount of shares as a typical investor of stocks, while only paying a small percentage of the money.

What Might Traders who are Less Savvy be Missing Out on?

Traders who are not as savvy may not know that they have this type of leverage. They may be unaware of the fact that they are already wielding this, and therefore choose to spend the same amount of capital that they would've spent establishing a stock position that is long, and turn around to invest all of it into a large position in options. The decision to go with options trading means that no one has to make unnecessary spending choices. One of the greatest benefits of trading using options methods is lessening risks and dangers, as opposed to multiplying them as other choices would likely do.

A great starting rule to start using is to hold back from investing more than five percent of your entire portfolio on any one, single, area of trading. Options trading does not just have to do with getting rid of risk to enjoy the equal amount of reward. Your goal here, instead of that, is to get the edge of a professional options investor. This means that you should try to get rid of risk using careful choices with your opportunities in investing while gaining larger returns at the same time.

A More Favorable Chance of Coming Out Positive:

Of course, there are going to be losses with this. But the ultimate goal of every trader is to change the amount of winners versus losers in favor of profitable and strong returns for the portfolio. All investing means is that you are accepting there is some risk involved in what you are doing. Investing with options has to do with larger risk, which means you should always make sure you are aware of all of the advantages and disadvantages of any strategy you might consider, before you begin trading at all.

In this section, we will cover the most common risks involved with investing options. As soon as you first option an account for options trading, your broker will give you a wider list of risks involved in options trading, as well as more details about each of them.

Some of the Most Common Risks for Trading Options:

- Time is against you, sometimes: No matter the option, it's going to expire eventually, and most of them do this at a completely worthless value. With investing in stocks, time is a positive, especially in terms of long options holding, but options trading is not this way. In fact, the closer to expiration an option becomes, the quicker the option's premium will go down.

This devaluation happens very quickly and goes even faster in the few days leading up to the official date of expiration. When you decide to be an investor of options, this should only be done using amounts of money you are comfortable with and can stand losing, since it's highly possible to lose everything at one time. Remember that using money you need is a highly unwise decision for options trading.

You can do These Things to Make Time an Ally instead of an Enemy:

-Purchase your Options when they are near or at the money.

-Only trade with options that have dates of expiration that encompass opportunities for investment in a comfortable way. - Purchase your options when you think volatility is undervalued, and sell them off when you think they are above value or overpriced.

Remember that Prices can Change Extremely Fast:

Since options are investments that are very leveraged, their prices can shift extremely fast. Prices for options can shift by huge amounts in seconds or minutes, rather than over days or hours, like stocks. People who are new to options should try to keep this in mind instead of assuming they will be the same as stocks.

How to Make Profit without Watching the Market Constantly?

Depending on the amount of time you have until the option expires, and the strike price of the option versus the stock price of the option, even tiny shifts can turn into huge movements in the option as far as its underlying value goes. Considering all of this, how can investors of options earn money without needing to be glued to a screen and charts every hour of the day?

A good answer to this is that you should find opportunities to invest in that make you believe the potential of the profit is so great that the price second by second won't be the main factor in the money making. In other words, chase profit chances that are large, meaning that the reward will be vast, even when it turns out your selling is not completely precise.

In addition to this, you should always do whatever possible to make the purchase of the option with the correct dates of expiration and strike prices, meaning that a lot of your risk gets lowered. Considering the tolerance you have for personal risk, it might be worth considering that you could close down your trades for option, leaving ample time before it expires, so that the value of time is not going down as drastically.

With Naked Positions that are Short, you can Suffer Big Losses:

Similar to short stocks, selling off options when you don't have hedging of your position with stock holdings or other options, also known as nakedly shorting options, could end up extreme losses. Naked short, referring to options trading, has to do with selling off calls or puts on their own, without having secured them with physical currency or another option or stock position. This could lead you to wonder what other ways you could sell off a call or put. Some investors will prefer the option of selling of calls or puts together with other options or another stock. This will take away the unlimited dangers that can result from naked calls or puts that are being sold off.

A lot of people in the investing world will use the term "short" in description of selling off option stocks to an open position, it doesn't mean the same as shorting the stock. When an investor does not go with the choice or shorting stocks, they are selling off stock that has been borrowed and is not owned. Eventually, you will need to give the stock back to its rightful owner, usually using your broker to do so. When it comes to options, you are not borrowing securities, but instead, taking over obligations that are tied in with selling off your options to receive the payment for premiums.

What Makes Volatility Selling so Appealing and What can Happen?

The quality that makes options naked, which can also be called volatility selling, appealing is that they offer a possibility of getting gains in a steady way. A lot of investing on a professional scale has gains that are booked from selling off options, since the stocks that are underlying were not as volatile as what was implied by the premium. There is a difference that must be noted between selling with the intention of opening up a call in a naked way, versus a put that is naked. If you are selling off a call that is naked, the risk you could endure is essentially infinite. This means you are in danger of the difference of how much that stock moves in relation to its price and the strike price. Since there's no limit to the amount the stock is able to trade at, the loss potential here is gigantic and never ending.

Potential Losses in this Area and Differences between Them:

But when you decide to sell this with the intention of opening a put in the naked way, the loss you can suffer means the difference of zero and the decided strike price. The risk for a sold put that is naked is essentially exactly the same risk that would come from owning the stock that is underlying at the same exact strike price. To put it another way, you cannot trade stocks under zero, so the loss you could suffer potentially is limited (or capped), but for some stocks that are priced high, falling down to zero could have the same effect as having unlimited losses.

Choosing to sell a put naked is possibly a great way to gain a lot of exposure to stocks at lower prices. You might have your eye on a particular stock, but it appears to always cost too much. Instead of chasing after the price of a stock, you can choose to sell, instead, a put, get the premium that comes from that, and turn long with the stock at the strike price you wish; if you see the share shift to the price. If you happen to be interested in the strategy itis called put-selling, you should always begin in a small way, at first. Get familiar personally with which outcomes may happen to you and then be sure, as always, to only invest what you can afford to lose.

How to Approach Trading:

When someone goes into options trading with their expectations set realistically and their eyes open, they will become much more effective at managing their risks and trades, in general. Once again, never put more than five percent of your funds for trading into individual chances or trades. This means that if it ends up turning in an unfavorable direction, you won't be completely devastated and have to quit trading altogether.

Another option for practicing trading without possibly devastating yourself is to use paper money, where you follow along with the market and take note of the steps you would have taken with real cash. Then your record your hypothetical "wins" and losses, along with what resulted in each. This will help you get better with what you know about investing, with no risk.

Chapter 5: Strategies and Techniques

As we've discussed earlier in this book, options are contracts that are conditional, and allow purchasers (also known as buyers or option holders) to sell or buy securities at a decided on price. Buyers of options purchase something known as a premium that grants them this right by the sellers. If the prices of the market happen to turn in an unfavorable direction for holders of options, they might allow their option to reach its expiration date and become completely worthless, which will make sure that their losses are not as high as or higher than the amount of their premium. Comparatively, sellers of options, also known as the writers of options, take on more risk than the ones buying the options, which explains why the premium is demanded for these transactions.

As explained in the first chapter, options consist of two segments, put and call options. The call variety consists of the one who purchases the contract buying the right to purchase underlying assets, at a non-determined amount, sometime in the future. This is also referred to as the strike price or exercise price. Put options consist of the purchaser gaining the right to sell off, at a non-determined amount, the underlying asset at some point in the future.

Why would someone Trade Options instead of Direct Assets?

Some distinct advantages exist in options trading, as compared with other choices. They allow traders to make strategies for options that range from easy or simple (relatively) ones that consist of just one option, to complicated options that have to do with many position possibilities existing at the same time. Now we will go over some basic strategies for options trading for those of you just starting out with it.

-The Long Call or Buying Calls: This is the position preferred by people who trade that do not wish to risk their money just in case a downtrend in the market happens, or that are bullish on specific indexes or stocks.

-Going for Leveraged Earnings in a Bearish Scenario: You can view options as instruments for leverage, meaning that they let traders play up benefits of putting smaller amounts of money at risk than would usually need to be risked if it were just the underlying asset being traded. Single stock standard equals 100 shares of equity. When you trade options, as an investor, you are able to leverage your options. For example, a trader may wish to invest a certain amount in a company, setting a price for each share. With the amount decided on, they can buy as many shares as possible for the determined price. Then, say the stock price goes up 10 percent. Not considering any fees for transaction, commission, or brokerage, that investor's portfolio will go up, allowing them to earn a return on their invested capital.

Considering the available budget for the trader, they can purchase however many options have just come into their budget with that money. However, this does not come without some measure of risk. The loss potential for the trader of using a long call will only be what the paid premium was. The profit potential is absolutely limitless, which means that payoffs could increase right along with the increases in the underlying asset.

-Long Put or Buying Puts: This position is preferred by investors who are taking a bearish position on a return that is underlying but don't wish to take on the danger of adverse motions in strategies that are based on short selling. This position is also preferred by people who wish to get the most benefit out of a position that is leveraged.

When a trader becomes bearish in regards to the market, it means he is able to short sell assets (such as Netflix). But, on the other hand, purchasing a put option can be another strategy for their shares. Put option choices will let traders have advantages from positions where a stock price fails. However, if the price does go up, a trader can then allow their option selection to become worthless by going past its expiration date, only losing out on their premium.

-The Covered Call Position: This position is usually taken by traders who are not expecting any changes or are prepared for the slight increasing of the price that is underlying. It is also typically for investors who wish to limit the potential of upside movements, and accept limited protection against downsides in exchange for that.

This strategy has to do with short positions involved with a call option, along with, in the underlying asset, a long position. The latter makes sure that the writer of the short call material must make good on their agreement to deliver the price of the underlying, if the long trader chooses to use (exercise) that option. With the option to use an out of the money stance, the investor can collect on some premium, although usually a small amount, allowing, also, for upside potential in a limited way. The premium that has been collected will cover losses of the potential downsides to at least some degree. All in all, this strategy copies, synthetically, the option of going for a short put position.

-The Protective Put Position: This is a state that is best for traders that are wishing for downside protection because they own an asset that is underlying. The protective put strategy has to do with the underlying asset's long position, along with an option position for the long put. Another strategy that could be used is selling off an underlying asset. However, at that time, a trader might not wish to liquidate, which affects the overall state of their portfolio. This could be because they expect to gain a high amount of capital over the course of time or in the long term and are wishing to get more short term protection.

If underlying prices go up as they mature, the option will pass its expiration date and become worthless, meaning that the trader will lose their premium. However, they will still have an advantage in regards to the underlying price of what they are holding going up. If the underlying price goes down, in another situation, the position of the portfolio of the trader will lose some of its value, but this will be made up for by what they gain using a put option strategy, used in specific scenarios and under certain circumstances.

Therefore, the protective put stance could be considered as a form of insurance. A trader is able to set their price for exercise under what the current price is at and lower the payment for premium, in exchange for having less downside protection. You could think of this as insurance that is deductible.

In Summary of This Chapter:

Options trading gives wonderful choices for alternative strategies, allowing people who invest to earn profit off of trading securities that are underlying. There are many different strategy possibilities that come from combining different options, derivatives, and also underlying assets. Simple strategies that beginners can use involve purchasing call, purchasing put, selling off, and when possible, covered call. Although these are effective as beginner strategies, to go beyond this takes a lot more knowledge and particular skills about derivatives.

Of course, there are benefits to trading options instead of focusing mainly on underlying assets. Some of these benefits are leveraged returns and protection for downsides. However, it is worth considering that some disadvantages exist too, such as needing to put down a payment upfront on a premium.

Conclusion

Thank you again for buying this book!

I hope this book was able to help you to have a better understanding of what options trading is. It is my hope that this guide was able to get your foot in the door of the world of options trading, and give you an idea about whether it is something you would be interested in pursuing. Although it seems intimidating at first, everything becomes easier to understand the more you become familiar with the concepts and terms behind it. This, in combination with plenty of research about strategies and risks will make you into a pro in no time.

While this book is a great starting point, you should always do as much research as you can with anything related to stocks or investing, so that all of your decisions can be informed as much as possible. Although some believe that this field is reserved only for the math whiz types of geniuses, that isn't true at all, and anyone can learn who is willing to try and practice.

By deciding to get involved with options trading, you will be taking the first step to enjoying financial freedom, greater savings, and perhaps even the chance to retire early. You will be giving yourself the choice to spend more time with your family or doing the things you love instead of constantly worrying about money. If this sounds good to you, by all means, pursue your options trading career with everything you have.

www.ingramcontent.com/pod-product-compliance
Lightning Source LLC
Chambersburg PA
CBHW071831200526
45169CB00018B/1309